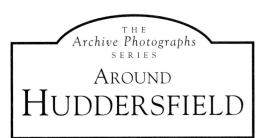

THE
Archive Photographs
SERIES
AROUND
HUDDERSFIELD

Milnsbridge *c.* 1930. A haze of smoke hangs over this landscape of blackened chimneys. These industrial areas generated Huddersfield's reputation as a producer of fine cloth.

THE
Archive Photographs
SERIES

AROUND
HUDDERSFIELD

Compiled by
Iris Bullock and Denis Broadbent

CHALFORD

First published 1996
Copyright © Iris Bullock and Denis Broadbent, 1996

The Chalford Publishing Company
St Mary's Mill, Chalford,
Stroud, Gloucestershire, GL6 8NX

ISBN 0 7524 0385 0

Typesetting and origination by
The Chalford Publishing Company
Printed in Great Britain by
Redwood Books, Trowbridge

Market Square *c.* 1902. If you were lucky enough to be in line for a new pair of boots, Freeman Hardy and Willis was the place to go. The latest footwear was on sale with prices ranging between 3s 11d and 6s 11d.

Contents

Acknowledgements

We would like to extend our thanks to Mr Roy Brook,
whose knowledge on early transport was invaluable.
Thanks to Carol, Betty and Peter for additional help
and information, also Lindsay Wills our typist.
We have endeavoured to supply some information on each picture.
For any errors we might have made we apologise in advance.
Finally we would like to record our appreciation
of those early photographers and publishers.
Without them we would not have had the pleasure
of collecting and compiling this book.

Introduction

Just over a hundred years ago the Post Office granted a licence to private publishers. This licence allowed the publishers, to produce picture postcards which could be sent through the post and very quickly sending and collecting picture postcards became a national pastime. All kinds of designs were introduced, amongst them real photographic views of towns, villages, railway stations and social events. These cards were often carefully stored in the family album, then left to gather dust as tastes and fashions changed. Now the surviving pictures are eagerly sought after by today's postcard collectors, as well as by people with an interest in social history. Whenever old photographs appear in newspaper features, they always produce interest and debate. Using some of those early scenes it is our intention to try to present a pictorial record of what life was like in and around Huddersfield approximately 100 years ago. At that time much of the town's wealth was centred on heavy industry, chemicals and textiles. Images of smoky mill chimneys standing guard over rows of solid terraced houses often appear, while the owners of these mills and factories lived in elegant Victorian residences away from the sooty air.

The town centre has inevitably seen changes over the years and many people still regret the demolition of some buildings such as the market hall and the Theatre Royal. Even the old Cloth Exchange, although perhaps not a beautiful building, would seem to have deserved a permanent place in the history of Huddersfield. Because shots of the main streets have often appeared in earlier books we have tried to look for the more unusual pictures here, this has often meant moving out into the surrounding villages where perhaps the scenes reveal even more about life in the early 1900s.

Long before the days of supermarket shopping each village had its own supply of shops. The staff were quite happy to pose outside seemingly well-stocked windows. The co-operative stores were well established and in 1905, the latest

Buxton Road shops opened, complete with a clock tower costing £320. Almost every village had its own carnival or school feast. For these days everyone wore their best clothes to follow the band in a parade round the village. Photographs show beautifully dressed children, the girls in starched pinafores, boys with fashionable sailor collars, and almost without exception a hat or cap of some sort.

In the town centre large crowds attended all the social occasions such as the Jubilee celebrations, dedications of some of the town's statues or Royal visits. More serious events were also recorded, such as Election results in 1910 and troops leaving to go to war. Disasters of all kinds were never far away and the cameraman was quickly on the spot to record these scenes.

Having a picture taken in the early days meant standing still for quite some time, which could account for the serious expression on many faces! Another problem relating to this was the half-vanishing figure, caused by someone moving out of shot before the exposure was complete. In spite of all these difficulties the early photographers are to be congratulated for the quality of the prints. We have enjoyed collecting these pictures and hope to give our readers some pleasure by sharing them.

One
Early Days

The old Parish church, built in 1506 and destroyed by fire in 1834. The perimeter walls were often used as a makeshift cloth market by local weavers, many of these clothiers would walk several miles with pieces over their shoulders, hoping to sell their wares to the merchants. This picture was reproduced around 1900 by Cooks publishers.

New Street, 1905. Amongst the buildings in the square are the offices of Cooks. This company was amongst the early publishers of picture postcards.

POST CARD

THE ADDRESS ONLY TO BE WRITTEN ON THIS SIDE.

Mr. W. H. COOK,

Artistic Stationery Works,

HUDDERSFIELD.

Cooks business card, 1892. Prepaid cards such as this were purchased from the post office, printed up and sent out to customers, in this case to encourage orders for private Christmas cards.

Woodsome Hall, *c.* 1910. Formerly the home of the Kaye family, at the time this picture was taken, the hall was the country seat of the Earl of Dartmouth. Since around 1911 the house has been occupied by Woodsome Golf Club.

Woodsome Hall, *c.* 1850. An artist's impression, this is a remarkably accurate portrayal when compared to the later photograph.

The Courtyard, 1850. Another reproduction, perhaps these would be the servants' quarters or a stable block.

The Banqueting Hall. Pictures giving a glimpse of life inside Woodsome are quite unusual. The grand fireplace with carved mantelpiece would be necessary to heat this large room.

Town Hall, c. 1926. The entrance to the Town Hall. In its early days this half of the building was used as municipal council offices, the words 'rent' and 'rates' can still be seen etched into some of the windows.

Town Hall c. 1907. This time viewed from the Co-op building showing the ornate canopy over the Princess Street entrance to the concert hall. The smaller canopy on Corporation Street can also be seen.

Market Square *c.* 1903. The Jubilee fountain was presented to Huddersfield by Sir John Ramsden in 1888, it was later moved to Greenhead Park. The buildings in the picture are virtually unchanged, but have had many different uses over the years.

View over Southgate Inn, *c.* 1910. It is difficult to work out the location of the cameraman, but it is most likely the Parish church tower. Industry, the gas works and housing stand shoulder to shoulder. This view is now altered beyond recognition.

Park Drive, 1910. An example of elegant homes of the professional and upper classes, enjoying uninterrupted views over Greenhead Park. Away from the sooty factory air these houses have stood the test of time.

St Pauls Street, *c.* 1904. Good quality middle class housing, rather grimy but well maintained, was condemned and demolished to make way for the polytechnic. Just visible in the right hand corner of the picture is the Drill Hall which was retained.

Huddersfield.

John William Street.

The Wrench Series, No. 6364

John William Street, *c.* 1903. Although the buildings are unchanged the photograph gives a rather deceptive view of the street. The right hand corner housed tea and coffee merchants.

RAILWAY STATION, HUDDERSFIELD.

W. COATES, HUDDERSFIELD.

The Railway Station, 1900. Peel's statue stands in front of the subway which used to be the entrance to platform 6. The station frontage is Huddersfield's only grade 1 listed building remaining within the town centre.

Old Bay Hall, *c.* 1900. This old Hall probably dated from around 1565, and was once the home of the old Brook family. It has substantially altered over the years but is still recognisable.

The Old Cherry Tree, 1890. Standing on the corner of Market Street and Westgate this inn was pulled down in 1900 and made way for the new Cherry Tree Inn. The corner was cleared again in 1931. Note the ghost – someone got tired of standing still until the exposure was complete.

The Bull and Mouth Inn, *c.* 1908. Published by Bamforths these were real photographic backgrounds with figures superimposed onto the picture. The inn was a notorious ale house, and one of the characters could be Alf Foy who appeared on the bill at the Palace Theatre.

BUSINESS IS ROTTEN

St Georges Square, *c.* 1908. Another Bamforth special, a rather out of proportion muddle of transport, all heading in different directions – anything for a laugh.

Huddersfield Royal Infirmary, *c.* 1901. An early picture of the infirmary shows the grand entrance, for the use of doctors and VIPs. The patient's entrance was around the back.

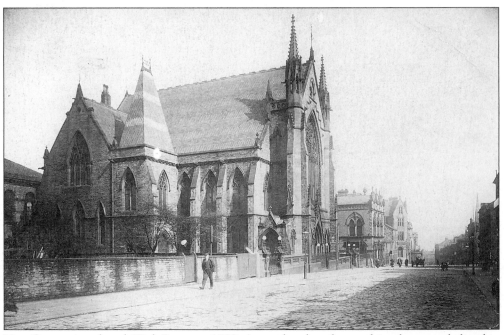

New Connexion chapel, High Street, *c.* 1900. A popular place for worship when people lived in the town centre. It eventually became un-economical around 1945 and ended its days making way for a modern shopping block, now partially occupied by the gas board.

Two
Events and Occasions

Royal Infirmary, *c.* 1912. Dedications of King Edward VII's statue. Matron and staff have the important positions, whilst a small group, almost hidden by the trees could be the patients. We presume the large potted plants were just to improve the picture.

Dinner Hour Meeting of the Open Air Mission at the Old Market Cross, Huddersfield

It is difficult to give a date for this mid-day meeting in the Market Place. Several intense looking ladies seem eager to save a few souls. The market cross makes a good 'speakers corner'.

I.L.P. CONFERENCE, EASTER MONDAY, AP 20TH 1908, TOWN HALL, HUDDERSFIELD

Labour Party Conference, c. 1908. Politics appears to be a serious business, judging by the sombre faces and mounds of paper in front of each delegate. The well attended gathering was held in the Town Hall. Does anyone recognise the famous faces of the past?

Beast Market, c. 1905. A large crowd gather to watch the lifeboat being pulled through the town centre. Probably a money raising event, but how did this large boat arrive in Huddersfield? It would be a long haul across the country.

Greenhead Park, 1905. Waiting to be unveiled is the Fallen Heroes Memorial, dedicated to the soldiers who fought in the Boer War. A very formal event, judging by the number of tall top hats.

ALLEN HEROES' MEMORIAL. UNVEILING CEREMONY. PHOTO LONGLEY &

Trinity Street, 1905. Preceded by the mace bearer, the official party enters the Greenhead Park. The unveiling ceremony was carried out by General French. Both volunteers and regular soldiers were honoured by this memorial.

Great Yorkshire Show, 1904. This site is now occupied by ICI-Zeneca along Leeds Road. Advertisements for several different railway companies can be seen in the background together with something called 'Waterloo round cakes'.

Upperhead Row, *c.* 1930. We cannot be certain of the purpose of this parade, possibly a money raising event for the Infirmary. The buildings on the right were pulled down to make way for the bus station. This is a rare glimpse of a once popular corner, 'Sparrow Park'.

Jubilee Tower, 1899. Built by Grahams of Huddersfield to celebrate the sixty year reign of Queen Victoria. The opening ceremony was performed by the Earl of Scarborough. In later years the height had to be reduced but the view from the top is outstanding.

Naggs Head, *c.* 1915. It must have been difficult to ride a bicycle in a dress like this. This picture shows the outside of one of the district's popular inns.

Isle of Skye, *c.* 1910. The Isle of Skye Inn was a well known landmark, situated on the moors above Holmfirth. At one time following the hounds on foot was a popular countryside pastime.

Lower Cumberworth, 1911. Many people will remember their own village feast. A day for wearing best outfits and following the band, the fun came later. These children look to be ready to sing. How did they persuade little boys to keep those enormous hats on their heads?

Golcar Sing, 1905. Present day Gala organisers would love to get a capacity crowd like this one. The site is the Golcar cricket field, background buildings include Cliff Ash, now the Colne Valley museum.

Ladies' Day Out, *c.* 1925. A group of unknown ladies having a day out in Bridlington. No doubt they would return still neat and tidy, we're not so sure about the men in the next picture.

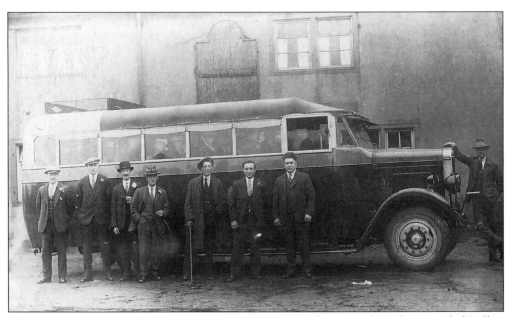

Gentlemen's Day Out, *c.* 1920. A real group of characters departing from the Spangled Bull at Kirkheaton.

Hillhouse, *c.* 1904. A detachment of Huddersfield Yorkshire Dragoons setting off to camp. Departure point was the old railway sidings, no longer used, the area awaits redevelopment.

Railway Station Forecourt, *c.* 1914. Steam waggons from B. Mellor and Sons, Holmfirth, seen here helping with the transportation of troops.

Hillhouse Lane, 1910. A rather overcrowded boat trip, believed to be a chapel outing from St Andrews Road, Turnbridge. This was a barge not a narrow boat, so it must have been going to Aspley Basin or towards Mirfield.

Three
Scenes and Streets

St Georges Square, *c.* 1900. A quiet scene looking across the square. A steam tram can be seen making its way into the picture. As the tram system was electrified around 1902 this must be quite an early photograph. On the right is the statue of Sir Robert Peel.

New Street, c. 1907. Almost traffic free, the trams were a sign of things to come. New Street has seen many different forms of transport and is now pedestrianised again.

Buxton Road, c. 1926. Another view, almost taken in the same place, but this time given a Buxton Road title. Policemen on duty here must have run the risk of having their toes run over on busy days.

Cloth Hall Street, Huddersfield. N° 11955.

Cloth Hall Street. Looking on the left of the street you will see the Huddersfield Banking Company headquarters with its mix of architectural styles, which later became the Midland Bank. Seen also is the clock tower above the market hall. Many people would have preferred these two buildings to have been preserved, but only pictures and memories remain.

Market Place. The market place has had a face lift, the public toilets have now become the focal point of the area.

845 New Street, Huddersfield.

New Street, *c.* 1925. Not too much traffic for the policeman to control. A nice view of the Waverley Hotel in the centre.

Queen Street, *c.* 1908, has almost a Dickensian feel. Note the unusual double edged pavement.

King Street, *c.* 1911. The lower end of this street is about to make way for the new Kingsgate Shopping Centre. Hopefully some of the old yards off the street will be preserved and renovated, to give a bit of character to the new development.

Chapel Hill, *c.* 1913. Old Bank chapel once stood on the right of the hill, now only the name remains. The small handcart pictured would be a vital piece of equipment for most tradesmen, as well as a strong apprentice to push it.

Cross Church Street, *c.* 1905. Flags give a patriotic feel to this scene. Products were often transported in barrels, this was the easiest way to roll and handle heavy goods. It almost looks as if this horse was pulling a double cart.

Ramsden Street Congregational chapel, 1908, is attractive, well built and prosperous. Like most chapels in the town centre its congregation declined as people moved further out of the town centre, it was pulled down to make way for the Public Library and Art Gallery. When it was built in 1825 it was considered very modern, as it had gas lighting.

Buxton Road, *c.* 1903. A rather faded view of the top of Chapel Hill. Many changes have taken place here, it has now become part of Huddersfield's busy ring road.

Co-operative Interior. Co-op stores existed in most of the villages in this area. Many of the goods for sale were manufactured by the CWS company. This restaurant was part of the Buxton Road central premises.

Buxton Road, *c.* 1912. The decorative canopy was the entrance to Victoria Hall, which was not a purpose built cinema, but one of the first places to show films in Huddersfield.

Buxton Road. The shops on the left have disappeared, amongst them, McKitricks ironmongers. A very functional shopping block has taken its place.

Cross Church Street, *c.* 1903. There is much of interest in this picture, taken outside the Ramsden Arms. Prams and bicycles are parked outside the shops, and a lone cow wanders along the street.

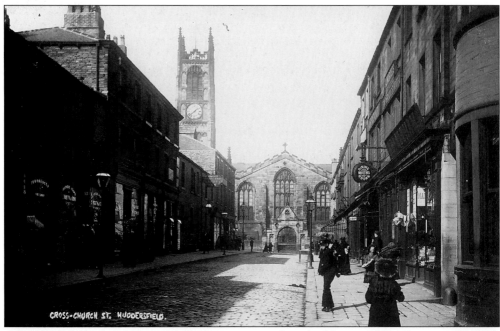

Cross Church Street, *c.* 1910. At this present time these buildings remain almost unchanged. Some are destined to become part of the Kingsgate development, but hopefully the best of the frontages will be retained.

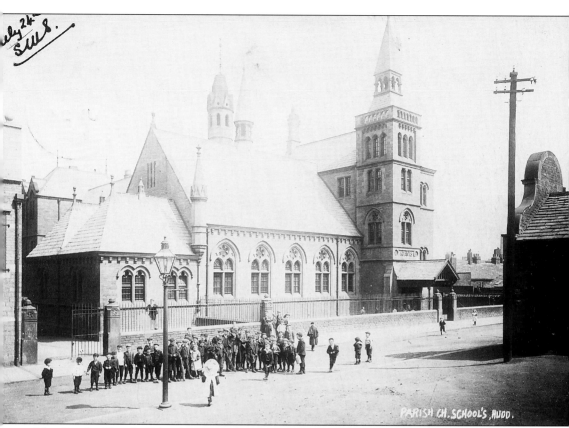

The Parish Church School, 1903. This is a very good photograph on one of the earlier Bamforth topographical postcards. Situated on Venn Street this gracious piece of architecture, with its ornate chimney will shortly be swept away. Children from the school pose happily for the camera. The block on the right was stables and court yard of a hostelry on Cross Church Street.

Prudential Building, New Street. Not many brick buildings of this age exist in Huddersfield. The style of the building was lost when the ground floor was converted to retail use. It was once home to the Prudential Insurance Company.

Queen Street South, showing the Technical School and Mechanics Institute which opened in 1883, and was the first purpose built technical college in the area. By 1915 it employed almost 80 full and part time staff. Over the years parts of the college have been housed in various buildings. Eventually most students were moved into the old Huddersfield Infirmary and new tower blocks.

Northumberland Street. The offices of the Tramway Company. According to ex-employees the regime was strict and unbending. Conversation during working hours was strongly discouraged, and two accounting mistakes in one week led to dismissal.

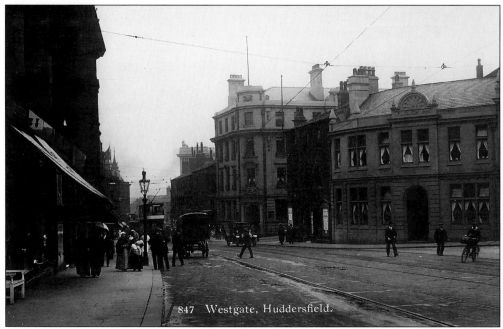

847 Westgate, Huddersfield.

Westgate, 1913. The frontage of the Plough Hotel is in sharp contrast to the soot stained Cherry Tree Inn next door. A rather unusual horse drawn waggonette waits on the left.

Westgate Huddersfield.

M. 522.

Westgate, 1919. A few years later the Plough has gained its layer of soot and now blends in. An often heard local saying is, 'where there's muck there's brass.' There was certainly plenty of soot.

Four

Industry

Beaumont Street, c. 1930. The evocative Beaumont Street Flyer crossing Northgate into Newtown sidings. Coal was taken from the sidings into the gas works and the spent coke returned. Young lads of the area would hitch a ride on the last trucks, if nobody was watching.

St Andrews Road, *c.* 1910. Hard work and rough equipment prepare a site for a new gas holder. The picture shows the radius arm, used for marking the circumference for the construction.

St Andrews Road, 1910. A different view of the construction work with the mechanic's workshop in the background. A steam powered excavator on its own railway lines straddles the trench.

Fitzwilliam Street, 1903. This building is Allan Haigh who were manufacturers of tarpaulins and rain proof coverings, extensively used for road and rail transport. The central building was probably the fore runner of Hopkinsons.

Northumberland Street, c. 1910. The old General Post Office. Pylons with only a few lines, would suggest the telephone service was very much in its early stages. The premises remain in use as general offices now.

Huddersfield Station Train Crash, 1905. This is a different view of the well documented train crash which happened on the Leeds side of the station. There are plenty of supervisors and viewers in spite of the danger.

Viaduct Street. Local tradesmen made full use of these arches; many traders allied to transport, farriers, coopers, and wheelwrights had premises here. Hence the need for the rather seedy looking gents toilet in the corner.

Northumberland Street, 1919. Sections of the tram track are being renewed at this busy triangular junction. It's possible to see the wooden blocks between the track, these had to be placed end up, and set in pitch.

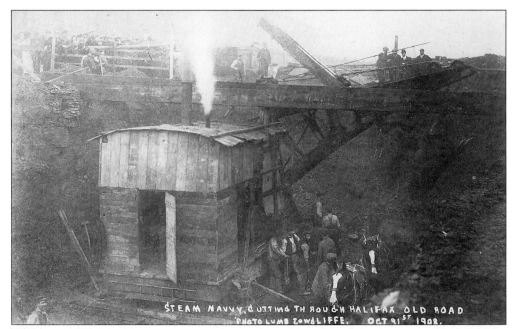

Hillhouse, 1908. More spectators, watching workers engaged on the construction of a bypass for Midland Railway. This would enable trains to run into Newtown sidings without paying to use the London and North Western lines.

Hillhouse, 1909. The line was eventually completed but did not have much use as the two companies shortly merged together. During the building work much use was made of brick rather than stone which was unusual.

Bradley Viaduct, c. 1912. This marvellous piece of civil engineering is now in a poor state of repair. It had to be built while ensuring the canal could still function.

Canker Lane. This is the temporary embankment and line which was used to transport the raw materials, needed to build the Midland Railway extension into Huddersfield.

Edmund Swallow, 1912. Ready to make a delivery is a horse and cart belonging to this manufacturer of hearth rugs whose premises were situated at Princess Street and 38 Leeds Road.

Taylor's Shire Horse. Joseph Taylor and Son, Kirkgate probably traded as steel factors. Their horse seems to have been decorated for some special event or carnival, it would perhaps be more at home hauling a heavy load of steel girders.

Canker Lane, 1912. A heavily laden barge makes it way towards Mirfield. Evidence of canal dredging is shown by the abandoned 'dumb' boat.

Viaduct Street, showing a horse and cart with the inscription H.B. Taylor, London and North Western Railway Company. The new metal bridge in the background was to enable public transport to pass under the viaduct.

Golcar Co-operative Shop. The most popular place to shop was the Co-op, with its promise of the 'divi' combined with a wide range of goods.

Birkby. Environmental health would have a field day with a scene like this. Meat must have been plentiful – if you could afford it.

Shepley Field Day. A horse and cart covering a round with fresh vegetables, would be a lifeline for many villages. The cart is shown here well turned out, for a gala day.

Steam Transport, E.H. Sellars. The exact location of this company is unknown to us. The coal looks to be kept on the roof, a silent powerful workhorse.

Starkey Brothers, Longroyd Bridge, *c.* 1904. Fires were always a hazard for textile mills. Spring Wood school and St Thomas church can be seen on the horizon.

W.C. Holmes, St Andrews Road. From early beginnings at Whitestone iron works, W.C. Holmes went on to become very successful gas plant manufacturers. The advent of North Sea Gas brought diversification and the eventual break up of the company.

Fire Station, Princess Street, *c.* 1900. An immaculate polished engine waits to be called out. Judging by the plants on the rafters, time between call outs was spent in horticultural pastimes.

Fire Engine. The steam pump would need to be kept simmering to be ready to go out and do its job. All the equipment was still horse drawn, at the time of the photograph.

Marsden Mill. These are possibly old Dobcross looms at J.E. Crowther's Mill. Old employees would remember the deafening noise of a weaving shed. The greenery must have been brought in to soften the harsh environment. Clever operators would switch off the machine and catch the shuttle before it banged into the box. This speeded up the process but was very dangerous.

Shepley. Not a lot of clues as to the whereabouts of this picture but we are told it is a Shepley mill and the name Will Auckland is written on the back.

J.E. Crowthers, Marsden. This is a group of tired looking textile workers. Hard work, without much pay earned them the nickname 'Povert Knockers'. The mill owners, the Crowther family were well thought of in Marsden and had a reputation as good employers.

Kirklees Mill. This is a faded, but rare picture of the old corn mill, and the fulling mill which both stood on this site between Cooper Bridge and Brighouse. The sixteenth century corn mill was water powered by three large wheels, one has been partially restored and survives today. The corn mill is now an attractive restaurant. But nothing remains of the fulling mill.

Five
Past and Pastimes

Kirklees Hall. For several centuries this historic hall was the home of the Armytage family. Sadly it now stands empty, awaiting redevelopment and a new use. The extension looks quite new at this time, a date of around 1910 is likely.

The Dumb Steeple, *c.* 1910. A short distance from Kirklees Hall stands this ancient monument. It was once a meeting place for the Luddites, who set out from this point to raid Rawfold's Mill in 1812, about a hundred years before this picture was taken.

Robin Hood's Grave. Situated on the hillside above Kirklees, is this grave, now overgrown and difficult to find, it is one of several graves claimed to be the final resting place of Robin Hood. The fenced tree was planted by Princess Louise on a visit to Kirklees Hall.

Tombstone. Another piece of evidence of Robin's grave: well preserved, if it has stood for seven centuries.

Old Priory. In Kirklees park was an old priory. This room in the priory is supposed to be where Robin died. The picture was reproduced in 1905.

Longley Hall pictured before its conversion to a High School for girls. This was the home of the Ramsden family, who owned most of the land that was to become today's Huddersfield.

Fireplace. One of the fireplaces in this well cared for building. The initials of the family are carved into the surround.

Old Coach House. Away from the main house was the coach house and servants' quarters. They are seen here in use as craft and woodwork rooms on the left, a gymnasium on the right.

Trinity Street. Standing to the front of Trinity church is this building, at this time in use as a private nursing home.

Theatre Royal, 1881-1961. Another piece of history has been swept away in the name of modernisation. Many of the theatres in surrounding towns have been beautifully restored, but this one did not make the grade.

£4

THEATRE ROYAL
HUDDERSFIELD.
Monday, Feb, 27th, 1905.

SPECIAL MATINEE
Saturday, March, 4th.

Mr Cyril Maude's London Company
IN THE ENORMOUSLY SUCCESSFUL PLAY
'BEAUTY and the BARGE'
BY
W. W. Jacobs and Louis N. Parker.
From the Haymarket Theatre, London
By Arrangement with Mr FREDERICK HARRISON

FULL OF FUN, ROARS OF LAUGHTER.

" *The Cinema Star,"*
Shaftesbury Theatre

THEATRE ROYAL
HUDDERSFIELD

MONDAY, MARCH 8th, 1915

For Six Nights at 7.30.   Matinee : Saturday
March 13th, at 2.15
Theatre Box Office 11 to 4.   Evenings, 8 to 9.30.
Saturdays 11 to 2   Telephone 607

**SEBASTIAN   SMITH
CHARLTON   MORTON
JO   MONKHOUSE
HILDA   GUIVER
LESLIE   GRAHAM
ETHEL   CALLANAN**

Programmes showing who was on the bill in 1905 and 1915.

Picture House. Another place of
entertainment, the Picture House,
the site is now part of the Piazza.

This 1936 building looks very new and modern. It was an extremely well built cinema,
the demolition men complained it was one of the sturdiest constructions they had ever
pulled down.

Cloth Hall Street, 1910. Natural progression resulted in this circular cloth market becoming redundant. Merchants preferred to use samples to show their customers, this also kept their fancy patterns more exclusive, and less able to be copied. The valuable Market Street site was too good to be left standing idle and this link with the past was demolished in 1930.

Old Weavers Arms. This Leeds Road hostelry looks rather different from today's attractive inns, with their enticing food and flower boxes. Situated on the edge of the canal, near to the tram depot, it was very popular and survived until 1966.

The Three Nuns, Leeds Road. This historic inn was pulled down and a more modern version erected a short distance away. The name is linked to the nuns of the old Kirklees Priory.

New North Road, showing the statue of Edward VII which stands outside the old Royal Infirmary, looking across to the nurses' home.

Inside the Infirmary. Even the children's ward looks rather grim in spite of the aspidistras and flowers.

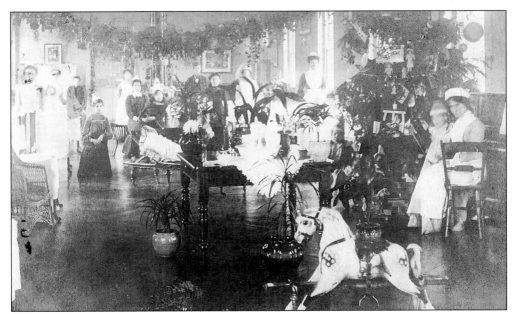

The Sanatorium, 1904. It is Christmas at the Sanatorium, there are good presents on the tree and lots of staff in attendance. Although there were several such hospitals, we think this might be Mill Hill.

The War Hospital, 1917. One of the many military hospitals needed to cope with the wounded of the First World War. The grounds at the rear of Royds Hall look to be the setting for this one.

Transport, *c.* 1910. Tram number 20 on its way to Marsh was capable of carrying 22 passengers downstairs and 32 up, with standing room for however many could get on. Built by G.F. Milnes this tram was scrapped in 1934.

Motor Bus No. 10. In the late 1920s experimental one man operation buses were tried out. Seen here with its wooden backed seats is the Jackson Bridge service. (Transport information courtesy of Mr Roy Brook).

Hillhouse Loco Dept, 1910. A tough band from the loco sheds formed a rugby team, not short of supporters and trainers.

Primrose Hill. Another football team, soccer this time, but still a serious pastime looking at their faces.

Six

Colne Valley

Marsden, 1904. This photographer has carefully composed his picture of these three gentlemen, posing next to the old stocks. The stocks have been moved during redevelopment and now stand opposite Towngate. The notice on the wall reads, 'J.W. Whitehead and Sons Tailors'.

Marsden, 1903. A nice clear view, looking over the railway and canal towards Pule Hill. Large, prosperous looking textile mills surround the village.

Crow Hill, *c.* 1915. The family home of the Crowther family, owners of the Bank Bottom Mills. Sent by a Bank Bottom worker to a friend, this picture postcard has the message, 'look at my Bosses house'.

Manchester Road. In the centre of the picture is the fire station, with its tower for practice and hose drying. Standing in the yard behind is a steam road roller, the barrels along the roadside are intriguing, but we have not discovered their usage. The picture would appear to be taken before the gas works was constructed.

Tunnel End, *c.* 1902, showing a canal maintenance boat belonging to the L.N.E.R. used for moving heavy cumbersome goods. In the background is a plank walkway for loading or unloading.

Argyle Street. Today this weir makes a nice feature in the centre of Marsden, but when built it would create a reservoir of water which could be diverted and used where needed. Some of the buildings have now been pulled down.

The Planks. This nostalgic view of cramped cottages shows possibly some of the oldest houses in Marsden. They have now been redeveloped and replaced with sheltered housing for the elderly.

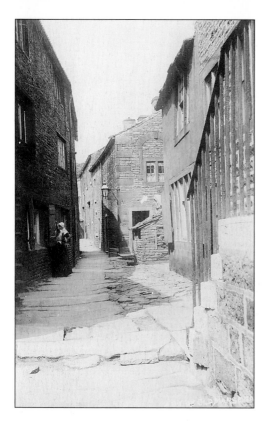

The Planks, 1907. Another view of the Planks, some of the cottages still have shutters at the windows. In spite of lack of facilities, they look tidy and cared for.

Hey Green, 1905. A rare photograph of the partly derelict corn mill. Nothing remains of the old mill nowadays, but the name is still painted on the warehouse at Tunnel End.

Crowther's Mill, *c.* 1900. There is an 'end of the week' look to this scene, quite a few of these textile workers have got smiles on their faces, and aprons bundled up ready for the wash.

Old Towngate. Now well known because of its use by the BBC, as the setting for Auntie Wainwright's shop, in the *Last of the Summer Wine* series.

Marsden church, 1905. An early picture of the church, still without its bell tower, which was added around 1910. Buried in the churchyard is Enoch Taylor, the Marsden machine maker, who unwittingly gave his name to the hammer used by the Luddites to break the cropping machines.

Marsden church, 1904. The church interior had just had a face lift with a new screen, choir stalls and organ balcony.

Waters Road, *c.* 1940. This is the road leading to Blake Lea, a popular picnic area. The reservoir which is partially silted up was used to top up water in the nearby canal.

Hopwood Farm. Formerly an upland sheep farm, it was later used as a youth hostel.

Peel Street. On the right is the entrance to the Mechanics Institute, which has recently been restored. The canopy is no longer over the shops, but the street is easily recognised.

Marsden Cuckoo, 1911. Like many of the villages Marsden had its share of characters and stories. This picture postcard illustrated one such story.

Colne Valley Election, 1910. Moving further down the valley, this is Slaithwaite Liberal Club, where a crowd of people await the election results. The building with its balcony remains intact, but is no longer the Liberal Club.

Manchester Road, 1906. Playing in the middle of the road was not unusual in these days, with only the occasional tram to worry about. What a collection of home-made carts is here to have fun with, or to be useful for collecting coal, firewood or even horse manure, as shown in another picture.

Slaithwaite Equitable Industrial Society. A grand title for an equally grand building. It looks a little sad nowadays with its roof and towers sliced off and replaced by a flat roof.

Slaithwaite Centre, *c.* 1906. Road, river and canal surrounded by mills and tall chimneys, this was Slaithwaite in the 1900s. The central building was the City Tea Company's grocery warehouse. The proposed reopening of the canal is still a controversial issue for many local residents.

Britannia Road. Not difficult to recognise, even though this shot must have been taken about 60 years ago.

Slaithwaite, 1905. Or 'Slawit' as it was sometimes called. The church is roughly in the middle of the photograph with the railway behind.

Slaithwaite church, *c*. 1905. A strong solid church, with some wonderful woodwork inside. Often difficult to keep warm, the congregation had to be tough and resilient like the building.

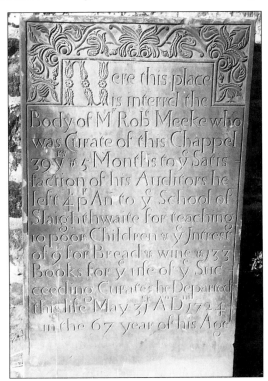

Memorial Stone. Close to the church wall is this stone commemorating a highly regarded clergyman.

Slaithwaite Station, 1905. The station with its four tracks and four platforms looks well cared for. Now it has become derelict and replaced by a wooden platform and a bus stop style waiting room.

Slaithwaite, 1905. This little coal office, once occupied by J. and J. Sykes Coal Merchants, is still there. At the moment it is boarded up, and awaits a new use.

Linfit Hall. Seen here in 1905 the Hall was surrounded by open country side. Now a busy road passes in front, and today's needs have taken away its tranquil setting.

Linthwaite, c. 1940. A general view over the valley, showing the rear of Linthwaite Hall now surrounded by housing, and no longer a country mansion.

Manchester Road, *c.* 1910. Information on the back of this picture tells us that the gentleman is Harold standing outside his shop, and his wife is at the gate of their house next door.

Linthwaite, 1907. In the nurses' fete procession is the float from the New Inn at Linthwaite, made up by members of the Royal Foresters Friendly Society.

Wellhouse, 1906. Clinging to the hillside, this small community is still quite isolated. Centre left is the village school, which is still in use.

Golcar, 1907. Golcar village on a clear day, in a quality photograph difficult to better using today's equipment. The church spire is an easily recognised landmark.

Swallow Lane, showing good, well built stone houses and the inevitable Co-op. A horse trough is still in place, and the telegraph pole has not many lines yet.

Church Street, 1932. Near the church is a public house, we think the name reads the Rose and Crown Hotel.

Victoria Road, *c.* 1907. Looking towards Primrose Hill, the industry in the valley is evident, with its dark satanic mills and houses to match. Nowadays it is a much greener, more pleasant place.

Milnsbridge, *c.* 1910. Here the valley widens out, but water and transport still keep the mills in the valley bottom. Squire Radcliffe's Mansion (of Luddite fame) still complete, is in the bottom left. The large mill has been replaced by Kwik Save supermarket.

Milnsbridge, 1907. There are people everywhere, all the windows are full of spectators, watching this parade. The staff of Firth's grocers have a good view, standing below the hams, hung outside the shop. These events were usually held to raise money for our local hospitals.

Milnsbridge. Here is another lovely photograph full of interest, this time of a Whit Monday gathering. Best clothes, polished boots and a few watch chains are in evidence. Wallace the grocers had a chain of shops around the district at this time.

Milnsbridge, 1922. Weavers' sheds with their steep, pitched windows, always face North, to get the best available light. Smoke pouring from the chimneys shows what a hive of industry this area was.

Milnsbridge. Tall mill chimneys standing guard over rows of terrace housing typify the era and the area.

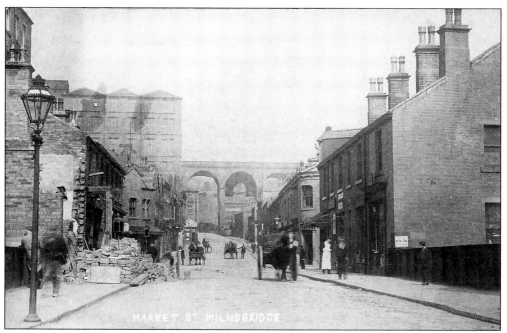

Market Street, 1910. Some kind of building or demolition work is taking place, possibly road widening, although transport seems to be still horses and carts down this street.

MAKING CONCRETE COVERING over RIVER COLNE, MILNSBRIDGE, YORKS.
ENGINEERS. MESSRS. ABBEY & HANSON, HUDDERSFIELD.
CONTRACTOR. MR. JOHN COOKE, HUDDERSFIELD,
CONCRETE MADE WITH KAYE'S CEMENT.

River Colne. Traditional stone is beginning to give way to reinforced concrete. Woodwork shuttering was becoming an important skill.

MILNSBRIDGE HOUSE, MILNSBRIDGE.

Milnsbridge House, *c.* 1915. Squire Radcliffe's house, seen here in almost its original state. This historic manor once housed Luddite prisoners in its cellars. Today it has been drastically altered, but the cellars still have an eerie feel to them.

Longwood Tower. Dominating the picture is the tower, built by unemployed people in the bad times after the war, to get themselves noticed, and to prove they could work. The occasional sing is still held there.

Longwood Gate. This is a sales cart belonging to Hobsons tobacco merchants. Their premises remained in High Street, Huddersfield until quite recently. This salesman meant to be noticed in this outfit.

Longwood Gate, 1904 showing Joseph Hoyle's Mill and adjoining cottages. Some people might remember the unusual overhead railway used to carry skips of bobbins. The brave driver sat in a cab suspended beneath the track.

Longroyd Bridge. Roof top view over St Thomas church and Harold Haigh's Mill. The open space was to become Brook Motors factory.

St Thomas Road. The motor car has now entered the scene and Manchester Road suddenly looks a busy main thoroughfare.

Seven

Towards Kirkburton

Moldgreen, 1906. A multiview which takes a humorous look at the local dignitaries and institutions of the time. The Conservative and Liberal Club are pictured, plus a notice saying Labour Club wanted. Did this reflect the political feeling of the time?

Aspley, *c.* 1903. Prominent in this scene are the premises of Bower and Child. This name regularly appeared on the old black leaded ranges found in local cottages. The windows had a good display of goods then, and still have, as they still occupy the same corner.

Green Cross Corner, *c.* 1904. Road widening meant this corner had to be demolished. Could this be Mr Whiteley standing so proudly outside his shop?

Star Hotel, Fenay Bridge. This pub stood just outside the old borough boundary, so it was very popular, because it could serve drinks half an hour later than the town pubs. A rare glimpse of Fenay Bridge Station is in the background.

Greenside Dalton, 1904. Wakefield Road is quite hard to recognise without many of today's houses. It almost looks as though the tram was stopped especially for the photograph.

Wormall Hall. This must be the most photographed building in Almondbury. Once the home of Isaac Wormall, it is presently used as the Conservative Club.

Almondbury, 1903. Before Penistone Road was constructed the main route to Huddersfield from Fenay Bridge was this road through Almondbury. Modern transport needs have altered the street almost beyond recognition.

Wormall's Yard. By contrast the yard behind, and former out building are not often seen.

Old Almondbury, *c.* 1901. Here is a bit of old Almondbury which must have vanished now. The lady has a rather overgrown garden to contend with.

Low Common, 1906. In this scene of peace and tranquillity, hardly changed today, only the hay ricks give an inkling that the scene is 90 years ago.

Lea Head Dalton, *c.* 1908. Swallowed up by the ICI complex, little remains of this road, which ran through from Rawthorpe to Nab Hill.

The caption on this picture says Old Black Bull, Kirkheaton, but we cannot find any record of such an inn. Next puzzle, the sign over the door says the Dalton Temperance Hotel; something of a mystery here.

Highburton, *c.* 1912. Showing the Old Market Cross, which is pictured outside the Smiths Arms. The base of the cross looks older than the precariously balanced ball on top.

Low Town Kirkburton. This is an almost perfect 'how we used to live' photograph. Carts like this would be used for all sorts of duties. Modernisation has taken place, but a lot of these houses remain.

Kirkburton, 1911. A sleepy cluster of cottages, where inhabitants were often woken late at night by the sound of a horse drawn load of shovels, rattling back from Wortley Forge to Carters Shovel works nearby.

New Brighton, *c.* 1910. A row of new looking cottages: was this why they were given the name New Brighton, or was it just a fashionable name in 1900? Plenty of livestock and produce are in the large allotments.

The Hallas. Outside houses built to last, both ladies are wearing their aprons; maybe it was a cleaning or baking day.

Parochial Excursion, 1912. A party from Kirkburton on a trip to Scotland. The exact location is unclear, but the hats certainly catch the eye.

Turnshaws. Except that its now extremely busy with traffic, this crossroads is little changed. Part of the Royal Hotel can be seen on the left.

Storthes Hall. Remembered as the 'asylum' by many, this large psychiatric hospital was almost a self contained village with shops, a farm and a cinema. In its busiest years patients were numbered in thousands.

Storthes Hall. More of the buildings on this vast complex. One of the corridors in the main building was supposed to be half a mile long. Here it looks quite new, including the landscaped beds.

Shepley Stone. The story handed down is that this stone was put on display, on the route to be taken by King George and Queen Mary after a visit to Penistone. Sadly, the Royal Pair were looking the other way and missed this effort. Amongst the party are Jonathan and Harry Lindley, Albert Adamson, Harris Wood and Hannah Day.

Shepley Co-op Jubilee, 1911. Gathered outside the Black Bull at Shepley a group of children in their best clothes wait for the celebrations to begin.

Abbey Road. Not much has changed during the last 80 years, only the road surface gives a clue as to the age of this picture, the buildings show little change. The light coloured building was the Stag Inn at this time.

Jos Lane, 1912. Just before the start of the First World War this was the scene at Jos Lane. This lane is very overgrown with trees now.

New Connexion chapel. No longer in existence, this chapel has been demolished, and replaced by a modern functional building.

Hampsons Quarry. If this stone weighs 24 tons it makes us wonder how they handled the 60 ton stone, shown in a previous photograph. Presumably the gentleman in the bowler hat was the boss.

Black Bull, Shepley. The members of this brass band are not wearing uniforms, but have bowler hats, which seems strange. The occasion is rather a mystery, but it's a nice group. How did the mothers manage to keep those boys clean, tidy and wearing those hats?

Eight
A Last Look Around

Folly Hall, 1904. This picture gives the appearance of a quiet back water, but over on the right the mill and smoking chimneys show the developing industry. In the years that followed, Folly Hall became an extremely busy working area. On a personal note, as a boy apprentice, I remember the effort that went into trying to be first in the queue at Thorpes chip shop, in order to get my dinner order before the boys from Jessie Lumbs.

Lockwood Brewery, 1905. A picture full of interest and detail, how did they manage to stack those barrels? The large amount of hay would be necessary to feed the shire horses used for pulling the delivery drays. It brings back memories of Town Major and Town Bitter – a man's drink.

Lockwood Bar, 1928. The corner outside Wallaces grocers shop used to be a difficult corner for the trams to negotiate. A few years ago, during road works, workmen unearthed the old tram lines which had been buried under the road surface. On the left is one of the trams made by the English Electric Co. Ltd at Dick Kerr Works, Preston.

Lockwood Bridge. Road widening has altered the bridge, and the White Lion has had a name change. Shops on the right have been demolished, but quite a lot of this picture is unchanged.

Berry Brow, 1904. Only Castle Hill in the distance confirms this as the road to Newsome. The railway bridge is still in place but virtually everything else has disappeared, including the rather nice gas lamp.

Newsome Road, *c.* 1903. Beautifully dressed children are gathered in Newsome Road. The adults also seem to be wearing quite formal clothes, could this be a church or chapel event? Another question is what is the purpose of the miniature walking sticks held by some of the children? This is a good clear photograph taken years before the Lounge cinema arrived on the scene.

Primrose Hill, 1905. One of the boys is holding a cricket bat, but hats and collars are still in place, suggesting not much play yet. The little shop on the corner has been neatly fitted in, to make good use of the available space. A scene taken near the Woodman Inn, this has completely changed now.

Oakes, 1904. The High Gate Oakes public house is on the left of the picture, together with a barber's pole and umbrella maker's sign. On the opposite side of the road, right up to the road side is Crosslands Mill. The mill had its coal supplies delivered into the yard by a special tram in the early days.

March, c. 1906. Gledholt chapel is just visible in the distance. The shops on the right have lost their forecourts, due to road widening but are still there, including what was the Co-operative building on the extreme right of the photo.

Outlane, *c.* 1910. Tram number 63 waits at the terminus, however the line did continue for a few hundred yards to allow the coal carriers into Joe Hoyle's Mill.

Outlane, *c.* 1910. A single line tram track leads down towards Huddersfield. Around this area was one of the last wheelwrights shops in the district.

Outlane, *c.* 1918. Outlane Golf Club once occupied the last two houses on the left hand row. Crossing the cobbles in spiked shoes must have been an acquired skill.

Oakes Pat Martin's Mill. It's not often a mill floor is seen empty like this, perhaps it was some form of refurbishment or installation of the sprinkler system, which is much in evidence. Information given suggests it was the mending room.

Nont Sarahs. This was the 'Orange Tree' trip to Nont Sarahs. There is nothing to indicate whether this is outside the pub but it looks likely. The man with the 'squeeze box' looks ready to play, and a few of the company look as though they have already sampled the ale. It could be a works outing sometime during the early 1930s or perhaps the lapel badges indicate some kind of benefit or sick club. Let's hope they enjoyed the trip.